NASCAR Champions
JEFF GORDON

Nicole Pristash

PowerKiDS press
New York

Published in 2009 by The Rosen Publishing Group, Inc.
29 East 21st Street, New York, NY 10010

Copyright © 2009 by The Rosen Publishing Group, Inc.

All rights reserved. No part of this book may be reproduced in any form without permission in writing from the publisher, except by a reviewer.

First Edition

Book Design: Michael J. Flynn
Layout Design: Kate Laczynski
Photo Researcher: Jessica Gerweck

Photo Credits: All images © Getty Images, Inc.

Library of Congress Cataloging-in-Publication Data

Pristash, Nicole.
 Jeff Gordon / Nicole Pristash. — 1st ed.
     p. cm. — (Nascar champions)
 Includes index.
 ISBN 978-1-4042-4446-7 (library binding)   ISBN 978-1-4042-4542-6 (pbk)
 ISBN 978-1-4042-4560-0 (6-pack)
 1. Gordon, Jeff, 1971– —Juvenile literature. 2. Automobile racing drivers—United States—Biography—Juv literature. I. Title.
 GV1032.G67P75 2009
 796.72092—dc22
 [B]
                                            2007046646

Manufactured in the United States of America
CPSIA Compliance Information: Batch# CR909101PK: For further information contact Rosen Publishing, New York, New York at 1-800-237-9932

"NASCAR" is a registered trademark of the National Association for Stock Car Auto Racing, Inc.

Contents

1	Meet Jeff Gordon	4
2	Big Winner	8
3	A Great Year	12
	Glossary	22
	Books and Web Sites	23
	Index	24

Jeff Gordon is a NASCAR driver. When Jeff was five, he helped build his own racetrack. He drove small race cars called **midgets**.

In 1990, Jeff began racing in the Busch **Series** of NASCAR races. He practiced a lot so he could get better.

Soon, Jeff moved up to NASCAR's top series. In 1995, he won the **championship**.

Jeff Gordon's car is a Chevy Monte Carlo. His number is 24. Jeff's car can go over 200 miles per hour (322 km/h)!

Jeff's practice and hard work paid off. He won many races. In 1998, he won 13.

Jeff is great at driving on road tracks. Road tracks twist and turn. They are **tougher** to drive than **oval** racetracks.

Jeff often takes time to meet his fans and talk with them.

Jeff Gordon does not always win. In 2005, he finished eleventh in NASCAR's **rankings**. Jeff pushed forward, though.

In 2007, Jeff won at Talladega Speedway, one of NASCAR's hardest tracks. He has become one of the best drivers in **history**.

Glossary

championship (CHAM-pee-un-ship) A meet held to decide the best, or the winner.

history (HIS-tuh-ee) A record, or list, of things that have happened in the past.

midgets (MIH-jets) Very small things.

oval (OH-vul) A shape that looks like a circle with two sides pressed in.

rankings (RAN-kingz) Guides to how well a player is doing in a sport.

series (SIR-eez) A group of races.

tougher (TUF-er) Harder than something else.

Books and Web Sites

Books

Jacobs, Paul DuBois and Jennifer Swender. *NASCAR ABCs*. Layton, Utah: Gibbs Smith, 2007.

Kelley, K.C. *Champions! of NASCAR*. Pleasantville, NY: Reader's Digest, 2005. Tradition Books (2002)

Web Sites

Due to the changing nature of Internet links, the Rosen Publishing Group, Inc., has developed an online list of Web sites related to the subject of this book. This site is updated regularly. Please use this link to access the list:
www.powerkidslinks.com/nascar/gordon/

Index

B
Busch Series, 6

C
car(s), 4, 10
championship, 8
Chevy Monte
 Carlo, 10

D
driver(s), 4, 20

F
fans, 16

H
history, 20

M
midgets, 4

N
number, 10

P
practice, 12

R
races, 6, 12
racetrack(s), 4, 1
rankings, 18

T
Talladega
 Speedway, 20

W
work, 12